Finding Out About
LIFE IN BRITAIN
IN THE 1970s

Pamela Harper

B.T. Batsford Limited, *London*

Contents

© Pamela Harper 1988
First published 1988

Typeset by Tek-Art Ltd, Kent
and printed in Great Britain by
Richard Clay Ltd,
Chichester, Sussex
for the publishers
B.T. Batsford Limited,
4 Fitzhardinge Street
London W1H 0AH

ISBN 0 7134 5672 8

Frontispiece
Silver Jubilee street party, June 1977.

Cover illustrations
The colour photograph is of Queen Elizabeth
on "walkabout" during her Silver Jubilee
celebrations in June 1977; the black and white
picture on the left shows a bomb scare notice
put up in Bromley Public Library in the 1970s;
the photograph on the right shows a Simplicity
dress pattern, typical of a particular fashion in
the 1970s.

Introduction

It is difficult for most people to consider the 1970s without comparing them unfavourably with the previous decade – the "Swinging Sixties". Whereas many tend to remember the spirit of optimism and change that was present throughout the 1960s, their memories of the 1970s are often of the fuel crisis, power cuts, the three-day working week, strikes and political confrontation. This book will help you to understand that this is a rather generalized, superficial view of our recent history. The 1970s were indeed a sober reaction to the relatively carefree days of the previous decade, but it is important to put the period's particular problems into perspective by also recalling the positive changes that took place during those ten years.

The problems of the 1970s affected everyone in one way or another. When oil prices rose rapidly in 1973, the world economy was plunged into a deep recession. This caused prices in Britain to treble during the decade. Many people demanded higher wages to pay for these increased prices. The wage rises in turn helped to fuel inflation. Strikes by workers resulted in power cuts and the three-day working week early in the 1970s. Later, during the "winter of discontent" of 1978-9, some lower-paid unions caused social chaos as they withheld their labour in the hope of a higher wage settlement. Some people blamed Britain's entry into the Common Market for the increase in the cost of living.

Young people could no longer look forward to the certainty of full employment. This forced successive governments to introduce new youth training schemes. Re-training, redeployment, redundancy and early retirement became a way of life for many workers as the economic recession hit world-wide. People also had to learn about the new technological changes that were sweeping into every area of life and to consider how to make better use of their increased leisure time.

One positive development in the 1970s was a greater concern for the environment. The oil crisis made everyone more conscious of the importance of conserving energy and also of finding new power sources that would not pollute the atmosphere. Societies flourished to protect the vanishing countryside, to save endangered species, to stop all forms of pollution, to further the recycling of valuable raw materials and to preserve old buildings. Organically grown food started to become popular as part of a reaction against modern technological farming methods. Health food shops became a common sight in the High Street. Exercise, especially jogging, proved to be more than just a passing craze as people realized the link between fitness and good health. Some activities such as yoga and meditation offered a road to mental as well as physical health.

A nostalgic interest in the past became very fashionable in the 1970s. Old buildings were renovated instead of demolished and old houses were redecorated in their original style rather than being modernized. Antique-collecting became a popular and widespread pastime. An overall feeling that the past should be valued seemed to prevail.

The present to many people meant the "Computer Age" and all the technological changes that came with it. The microchip revolutionized life at home by providing us with more labour-saving devices. In industry, many production lines became more efficient as automation was introduced. Jobs were lost, however, as a result of this. Similarly, computers were installed in offices to carry out the work previously done by several human employees.

Other developments and events of the 1970s

included the birth in Britain of the first test-tube baby, the first commercial supersonic flight across the Atlantic and the celebration of the Queen's Silver Jubilee. Moves were made towards an increase in sexual and racial equality. Many teenagers identified with the New Wave Punk movement that brought exciting and outrageous innovations into the worlds of fashion and pop music. There were also many individuals who advocated change in other areas. You can read about two of them — Freddie Laker and Kerry Packer — in the chapters on Holidays and Sport.

Find out how the 1970s, with its problems, movements, events and campaigns, affected your family, home, school and local area. How did your relatives celebrate the Silver Jubilee or cope with the water shortage during the drought summer of 1976? Did your school close during the "winter of discontent"? How did your local shops manage to stay open during the power cuts and the three-day working week? Build up your own picture of the decade and judge for yourself whether it really was a reaction to the lively days of the 1960s, or rather more of a turning-point as an increasing number of people started to think and care more deeply about social issues.

Find football programmes from the 1970s. Look at the hairstyles of the players, the league divisions that the teams were in and the design and lay-out of the programme covers.

=Useful Sources=

1. PEOPLE

a) *Librarians*. The librarian in the reference or the local history section of your main public library will be able to show you what material the library has on life in the 1970s.

b) *Teachers*. Ask your teacher about education in the 1970s. Your head teacher may be able to arrange for you to see the school log book, or the minutes of parents' and governors' meetings. Your school may keep photographs showing how the children celebrated special occasions in the 1970s such as the Silver Jubilee. Copies of old school magazines may be kept in your school library.

c) *Relatives and friends*. Talk to as many people as you can about their lives in the 1970s. To get a good cross-section you need to talk to both young and old people. Many will still have clothes and furniture bought in the 1970s. Other sources that people may provide are magazines, records, scrapbooks, photographs, theatre and sports programmes.

2. VISUAL MATERIAL

a) *Maps*. The local library may keep maps of your area. Compare those of the 1970s with others of an earlier and later date. Look out for new roads and by-passes, housing estates, shopping and leisure centres and the redevelopment of town centres.

b) *Photographs*. Collections of local photographs are often kept in public libraries. Choose a particular area or event and ask the librarian to show you any relevant photographs. Local newspapers may also keep copies of photographs taken in the 1970s. Enquire at your local office. Find books about fashion, music, homes, or transport and look for photographs taken during the 1970s.

c) *Films and T.V. programmes*. Some T.V. programmes and many films made in the 1970s are repeated on television today. Watch them to find out about different life-styles, fashions, and trends in music and architecture.

9454 Simplicity 40p Inclusive P.T.

Clothes patterns such as this one from 1971 tell us not only about dress styles but also about fashions in footwear and hair.

d) *Objects*. Ask older friends or relatives to show you any objects that they bought during the 1970s. Look at ornaments, pieces of furniture, games and kitchen utensils. These things will help you to learn about fashionable design and popular trends of the decade.

e) *Buildings and museums*. After you have looked at the maps in your library you could wander around the local area to actually see the changes that took place in the 1970s. Things to notice include the building materials used, the height of new buildings, the renovation of old buildings and how some new areas were landscaped to make them more attractive.

The 1970s is still too recent a decade for many museums to have their own collection of exhibits. Why not start a museum or collection of your own at school? Your class could collect artefacts and display them to help others find out about the period.

3. WRITTEN SOURCES

a) *Books*. There is a list of useful books on page 47. Try to find some of these in your local library. Year Books and annuals provide a record of the events, personalities and developments of a particular year. You may be able to buy quite cheap copies of them from second-hand bookshops.

b) *Newspapers and magazines*. The reference section of your main public library may keep old copies of national and local newspapers (they may be on microfilm). The newspaper advertisements will tell you as much about life in the 1970s as the stories will. Local parish magazines can also be useful and may be available in your library. Ask the librarian if any other old magazines are kept by the library. Some people give their unwanted magazines to charity shops. In these, you might be lucky enough to find old copies of *Punch*, *Private Eye*, *The Illustrated London News* or *The Listener*, for example.

c) *Diaries, letters and memoirs*. Some famous people have published memoirs which include the events of the 1970s. Other people have compiled books containing the diaries or letters of personalities of the recent past. Look in the biography section of the lending library for copies of these books.

d) *Keesing's Contemporary Archives*. These may be found in the reference section of your main library. They provide a good summary of world events for each year. If you find the index difficult to use, ask the librarian to help you.

e) *Hansard*. This is a detailed record of all parliamentary debates. It should be available in large libraries.

f) *Council Minutes*. These can give you a valuable insight into the important local issues of the 1970s. They may be found in the library or at your Town or County Hall.

The first government of the decade (1970-4) was a Conservative one led by Edward Heath. One of its major pieces of legislation was that enabling Britain to apply for membership of the E.E.C. The Government had also to deal with two national miners' strikes – the first since 1926 – and an oil crisis which plunged the world economy into the deepest recession since the end of the Second World War. Confrontation with workers, especially the miners, contributed to the downfall of Heath's Government, which was replaced in 1974 by the Labour Party, led by Harold Wilson and, on his resignation in 1976, by James Callaghan.

CONFRONTATION

Confrontation with the miners in 1972 and 1974 had a dramatic effect on the life of the country. The Conservative Government was forced to declare a State of Emergency, and the three-day working week and regular power cuts were introduced. Television broadcasts ended at 10.30 p.m. each night. How did the public cope with these conditions?

> **On Monday, when the ban on electric heating in shops and offices came into force, office girls sat at their typewriters well wrapped in trousers, top coats and gloves – though the latter may have affected the standard of typing .... Nicholson's sold £700 worth of candles at 5p each in four hours last Saturday. Long queues formed as anxious customers took the opportunity to stock up .... Unlucky housewives caught under hairdryers during black-outs have had to beat hasty retreats from hairdressers to home wearing curlers and head towels.**
> (*Bromley Times*, 18 February 1972)

This Government began by giving way to union demands for higher wages. Government spending soared, as did inflation and public borrowing. By the autumn of 1976, the I.M.F. (International Monetary Fund) had to be called in to loan money to the Government and to support the economy.

Two bills allowing for separate assemblies to be established in Scotland and Wales were passed by Parliament. The bills included the condition that devolution of power would have to be approved by a referendum in Scotland and Wales, with at least 40 per cent of the electorate voting in favour. Both bills failed, winning only 12 per cent of the vote in Wales and 33 per cent in Scotland.

Following the "winter of discontent", the Labour Government was overthrown on a vote of no-confidence in the House of Commons, and the General Election of 1979 returned the Conservatives to power. As the new leader of the Conservative Party, Margaret Thatcher became Britain's first woman Prime Minister. With her came tough policies to reduce public expenditure and curb union powers.

NORTHERN IRELAND

Bitterness between Protestants and Roman Catholics in Northern Ireland erupted into violence in the late 1960s. British troops were sent there in 1969 to help control the situation. The Roman Catholic minority complained that they were discriminated against in the allocation of jobs and houses. The Protestant majority feared that Northern Ireland was to be reunited with the Catholic Irish Republic in the south. During the 1970s 2000 lives were lost as a result of these troubles, over 60 of them in mainland Britain. The I.R.A. (Irish Republican Army) is a Catholic terrorist organization whose aim is to achieve a united Ireland. It mounted several bombing campaigns in mainland cities during the 1970s.

'Arthur Egburt Miller (Conservative) two votes. I therefore declare that the said Arthur Egburt Miller is duly elected as member of the European Parliament for this constituency.'

In 1979 the first direct elections to the European Parliament were held. This cartoon from The Guardian *(12 June 1979)* satirizes the poor turn-out at the polling stations.

At least 17 people were killed and more than 120 were injured last night after bombs exploded almost simultaneously in two crowded public houses in the heart of Birmingham. No warning seemed to have been given for any of the explosions, which brought the highest death toll in England for an I.R.A. bomb attack . . . . Emergency services were called in from all districts surrounding the city as customers in the public houses, most of them young people, lay dead and dying. Those who survived the initial blasts – at the Tavern in the Town cellar bar and the Mulberry Bush – faced the horror of walls and ceilings falling on to the places where they lay trapped. (*The Guardian*, 22 November 1974)

EUROPEAN ECONOMIC COMMUNITY

On 1 January 1973 Britain became a member of the E.E.C. Some people thought that the Common Market was a good idea, as it would give Europe economic and political unity; others felt that the strong differences between the member states would deter unification. Much of the E.E.C. legislation was concerned with agriculture, and it was this area that caused most controversy.

At the moment all imports of beef from any country in the world into the E.E.C. are totally banned by the Brussels bureaucracy . . . . Meanwhile the Marketeers' own beef mountain – too dear for us members to buy – is now over 200,000 tons; and 8000 tons of it is stored in ships in Bantry Bay [southern Ireland] because the warehouses are full. But 30,000 tons has been sold cheap to the Russians again, and is on offer at subsidized low prices to anybody lucky enough not to be an E.E.C. member. (Douglas Jay in *The Spectator*, 28 September 1974)

Despite difficulties such as these, the Common Market gradually became accepted, as the result of the referendum (Britain's first ever) held in 1975 showed, when two-thirds of those voting favoured continued membership.

Ask older friends and relatives how they voted in the referendum and why.

People and Events

THE GREAT DROUGHT

The 12 months ending in April 1976 were the driest since records began, in 1727. Then, from June to the end of August, there was unbroken sunshine, with temperatures regularly over 25° Celsius. Reservoirs and natural waterways dried up, causing a severe water shortage. Public houses and shops selling soft drinks and ice-cream enjoyed a boom in sales, but the countryside became scorched and brown.

Jilly Cooper lived near Putney Common, London, in 1976. She describes the drought in her diary.

> *Friday July 2nd.* **The drought is getting critical. The Common is completely dried out. The chestnuts are dropping leaves as they would in Autumn.** *Sunday July 4th.* **We have all been forbidden to use the hose or the** sprinkler in the garden, which means I tear back and forth all morning with buckets and watering cans . . . . *Saturday August 21st.* **Wales has had its water cut off for 17 hours a day. Feel very guilty about watering the garden even with buckets.** (Jilly Cooper, *The Common Years*, Methuen, 1984)

On 26 August Denis Howell was appointed Minister with Responsibility for Water Resources. A few days later the rains began — and continued well into the autumn.

Find reports of the drought in your local newspapers. How was your local area affected by it? In what ways did your family try to save water?

Street parties like this one in Bromley, Kent were held all over the country in June 1977 to celebrate the Queen's Silver Jubilee. Did your family or school keep any photographs of their Jubilee celebrations?

THE TREASURES OF TUTANKHAMUN

In 1972 nearly two million people visited the British Museum to see the exhibition of the relics from the tomb of the ancient Egyptian boy-pharaoh, Tutankhamun. People queued for many hours in order to view the exhibits.

> **The dawn queue alongside the glowering black wall of the British Museum has an air of cheerful shipwreck. Transistors, picnic baskets, striped beach chairs and blankets are sustaining the survivors, and light-heartedness is breaking out. Only three hours to go before we're first in.** (*Evening Standard*, Tutankhamun Souvenir Issue, 3 June 1972)

Would you be prepared to queue this long for an exhibition? If so, what sort of exhibition would it be? Ask in your local library for books with colour photographs of the exhibits, especially Tutankhamun's gold mask; these pictures will help to explain why this exhibition was so popular.

Advertisements were placed in newspapers and magazines to inform the public about the new system of coinage to be launched on D-Day 1971.

D-DAY

Money was decimalized in Britain on 15 February 1971. This was known as "D-Day". Before that, some new coins had been introduced gradually, to facilitate the changeover. Not everyone was happy with decimalization.

> **Mr N. Grant, of Pollards in the Royal Parade, thought that the new system was a waste of time . . . . "Everybody is suspicious of it. It makes a lot of work for both customer and shopkeeper and I think the whole change could have been well left alone. A great deal of time is lost in explanation to the customers and others grow impatient at the delay."** (*Chislehurst Times*, 19 February 1971)

Many old people also found the new system confusing. Children, however, tended to adapt well, as they had already been dealing with decimal coinage in schools prior to D-Day.

Find out if your school has any copies of old Mathematics text books that contain problems using the old pounds, shillings and pence system. Try to solve some of the problems. (There is a conversion table on page 44 of this book.) Which system, old or new, would you prefer to use? Why?

THE DEATH OF MOUNTBATTEN

On 27 August 1979, the 79-year-old Earl Mountbatten of Burma was assassinated by an I.R.A. bomb in Ireland.

> **The nation saluted Earl Mountbatten of Burma yesterday with a ceremonial procession and a service at Westminster Abbey. Under a cloudless sky, watched in silent tribute by thousands, the military procession wound its way to the Abbey. The Queen led mourners at a service of dignity and splendour in the Abbey. Then Lord Mountbatten, described by the Archbishop of Canterbury as "so rare a person", was taken to his last resting place near his Hampshire home.** (*Daily Mirror*, 6 September 1979)

A large gathering of royalty – six kings, five queens, 21 princes and 18 princesses – attended the funeral service, which had been planned by Mountbatten himself, many years before his death. Try to find out more about his life and career.

Employment

The 1970s were unhappy years for many areas of British industry. High production costs, outdated machinery and competition from overseas all played a part in the decline of manufacturing industries. These problems were made worse by poor labour relations between management and workers. Areas of growth included the North Sea oil and gas industries, service industries and those concerned with high technology. These provided some new jobs but not enough to halt the upward trend of unemployment during the decade.

THREE-DAY WORKING WEEK

Industrial action (in support of a pay claim) by electrical power workers, miners and some railway workers, plus a cutback in oil deliveries from Arab countries, created an increasingly serious energy shortage in late 1973. On 13 December the Prime Minister, Edward Heath, announced that electricity supplies to most factories, shops and offices would be limited to three days a week. The following newspaper report describes how these measures affected some workers:

> **Mr Wilkins works in the stores (of Farnborough Engineering) and has been able to work some of the time during the power-less days, although of course, without heating and lighting. He estimates that his wages are about £8 a week lower than normal due to shorter hours and no overtime. Mrs Wilkins is a canteen assistant and is working only 3 days. She estimates her loss in wages at around £6. Mrs Wilkins said, "This is only our second week on short time and we have not really felt the pinch yet. Another month like this and we will really have to start cutting back."** (*Bromley Times*, 10 January 1974)

Copies of your local newspaper from this time will tell you how the three-day working week affected your area. Older members of your family may remember how they coped at home and at work without electrical power.

NEW TECHNOLOGY

The introduction of new technology, and in particular computers, was blamed by many for the increase in unemployment. The environmentalist Michael Allaby, however, maintains that microprocessors in fact created work:

> **Think of the numbers of people employed in the computer industries and making those control devices that did not exist at all a few years ago. The pocket and desk calculator industry is new. The digital watch and clock industry employs about as many people as used to make clockwork watches and clocks . . . . All that has happened is that humans are no longer required to perform tasks that are simple, repetitive, boring and unpopular, but are allowed to develop and exercise higher skills.** (*Here's Health*, September 1979)

Can you think why people who lost their jobs when their industries were computerized would not have agreed with this point of view?

Britain's membership of the E.E.C. made it easier for Britons to work in other Common Market countries. This advertisement appeared in the Daily Mirror (6 September 1979).

NORTH SEA OIL AND GAS INDUSTRIES

Oil from the British sector of the North Sea was first drilled on a large scale in 1975. Less than three years later North Sea oil was providing half of Britain's requirements and North Sea gas meeting 99 per cent of consumption. In addition to those workers employed in offshore exploration and production, many more people found jobs providing the materials and services needed to support the North Sea activities. Helicopter pilots, supply-boat crews and caterers were among those employed in related industries. A. Alvarez, the writer, describes the offshore workers and the jobs they left behind in the 1970s:

> **Many of them have come offshore from Britain's declining industrial regions. The factories where they once worked have gone bust and they have lost their jobs through no fault of their own. So they come out to the North Sea grudgingly, as a last resort, because the work is there and pays well.** (A. Alvarez, *Offshore – A North Sea Journey*, Hodder and Stoughton, 1986)

Why, do you think, were workers reluctant to go offshore?

UNEMPLOYMENT

Changes in the industrial structure of Britain resulted in a loss of jobs in the late 1970s and heralded the steeper rise of unemployment in the 1980s. By the mid 1970s there was a larger number of people of working age than ever before – the result of an increased birth rate in the 1950s and 1960s. This meant that there were too few jobs to go round. Many people were disappointed and frustrated as they looked for work.

> **I've been all over, but when I get there they say the job's been filled or have I got references. I'd like to do decorating but I'm a bit slow now. I'd do sweeping for the council, anything, but nobody wants me.** (Unemployed man quoted in *New Society*, 6 December 1979)

What is the official figure for the number of people out of work in Britain today? Why has the figure changed since the 1970s?

The first Jobcentres opened in 1973, replacing the old Employment Offices. They provide an open-plan display of job opportunities as well as personal help and advice. Find out about your local Jobcentre. How long has it been open and what services does it provide?

Unemployed men queuing for their dole money in Mortimer Street, London in June 1973. How was your area affected by unemployment in the 1970s? You could ask at your local Jobcentre or look for reports in old local newspapers.

Education

The number of pupils attending schools fell considerably during the 1970s. This led to the closure of some schools and the redeployment of teachers. Other schools were merged with each other. As a result of the economic recession less money was spent on education, and there was a call from some politicians to ensure that schools were providing value for money. Some critics claimed that standards were falling and that education was not keeping pace with the times. So-called "informal" and "progressive" teaching methods were often blamed for this. Much reorganization went on, with the establishment of more comprehensive schools and the first, middle and upper schools which operated in some areas.

COMPREHENSIVE SCHOOLS

Comprehensive schools, proposed by the Labour Government, were established in many areas in the late 1960s and early 1970s. Before this, pupils were allocated places at secondary schools on the basis of their results in an "eleven-plus" examination. Those who passed this intelligence test went to a "grammar" or "technical" school and those who failed went to a "secondary modern". Some Conservative councils and education authorities resisted reorganization, and in some areas the change-over to comprehensives was slow because new buildings were required. By 1980, however, 83 per cent of pupils in the state system were in schools organized along comprehensive lines.

Secondary Education in Bromley is to go comprehensive within five years from now. Bromley Council came down firmly in favour of comprehensive type schools at their meeting on Monday – despite a last-ditch stand by some Conservative members to defer or reject the plan. Critics of the proposal . . . alleged that the Council had been "blackmailed" into it by the Labour Government of that time. (*Chislehurst Times*, 19 February 1971)

How are secondary schools organized in your area? Are they run as comprehensives? Find out if your local council was keen on the idea of comprehensive education when it was first introduced. You could look in old local newspapers for reports or in the Minute Books of council meetings.

Find out if your school had to be closed for any reason during the 1970s.

OPEN UNIVERSITY

The Open University was set up in 1969 in the new town of Milton Keynes. It pioneered new teaching methods where degrees were taken largely by post. Students learn in their own homes, using "multi-media" techniques — text books and study packs, T.V. and radio programmes and video and audio cassettes. For the first time, students without formal G.C.E. qualifications were able to follow courses and gain degrees. By 1975, this "second chance" university had 50,000 students. *Educating Rita* is a play by Willy Russell about a young hairdresser, Rita, who embarks on an Open University course after an unsuccessful school career. (It has also been made into a film starring Michael Caine and Julie Walters.) Frank, a tutor of English at an ordinary university is Rita's Open University course tutor.

Rita Do you get a lot of students like me?
Frank Not exactly, no . . .
Rita I was dead surprised when they took me. I don't suppose they would have done if it'd been a proper university. The Open University's different though, isn't it? . . . .
Frank It's supposed to embrace a more comprehensive studentship, yes.
Rita Degrees for dishwashers. (Willy Russell, *Educating Rita*, Methuen, London, 1981)

MULTI-MEDIA LEARNING

During the 1970s schools began to use the multi-media techniques pioneered by the Open University. Today these are commonplace, but at that time they were revolutionary:

Anyone entering a school for the first time for a decade or so must be impressed by the range of learning aids available to the teacher. In addition to the traditional text-book, atlas and wall chart and the well-established gramophone, radio, and television receiver, there is likely to be some

PRIMARY SCIENCE

During the late 1970s concern was expressed by teachers and by people in industry that there was not enough good science teaching in primary schools. Science was often limited to looking at a nature-table display instead of learning scientific skills through practical experimentation.

Few primary schools visited in the course of this survey had effective programmes of the teaching of sciences. There was a lack of appropriate equipment; insufficient attention was given to ensuring proper coverage of key scientific notions; the teaching of processes and skills such as observing, the formulating of hypotheses, experimenting and recording was often superficial . . . . The most severe obstacle to the improvement of science in the primary school is that many existing teachers lack a working knowledge of elementary science appropriate to children of this age. (*Primary Education in England. A Survey by H.M. Inspectors of Schools*, 1978)

What form does your science learning take today? Ask your teachers if they can remember changes in science teaching. Is more practical equipment available now? Were new science projects introduced? Did they attend courses to help them teach science more effectively?

means of reproducing the printed word, ranging from a simple duplicator to a photocopier . . . . most schools now have tape recorders and video-tape recorders, and a few have some facility for producing television programmes. (*The Listener*, 14 October 1976)

Imagine learning without these new resources. How have multi-media techniques changed learning in schools? What is the major new learning resource of recent years?

Young People

In the 1970s teenagers started to worry more about their long-term employment prospects. Less money was made available from central funds for further education courses. Many employers were unable to take on young trainees as the economic recession hit their businesses. Schools began to prepare students for unemployment and increased leisure time as well as offer career advice.

THE DISILLUSIONMENT OF THE YOUNG

For many reaching their teenage years in the 1970s the promises of the previous decade failed to materialize. Sally-Ann Lomas, who was born in 1960, wrote this article in *The Guardian*:

> I grew up believing that to be a teenager was everything you could wish for in opportunity and fun . . . . In 1974 I was ready to hit the world . . . . But something odd was going wrong. The youth clubs, the theatre clubs, the dance halls and coffee bars were closing . . . . Pocket money didn't seem to stretch very far, Dads rebelled against ever-present demands for more, their pockets suddenly empty. Saturday jobs were scarce. And yet, the television told us, the radio did too, that to be young was "it" . . . . There was this strange perplexing gap between the image and the experience. (*The Guardian*, 27 August 1986)

What were the reasons for this gap? Are there more opportunities for the teenagers of today?

Despite poor job prospects, young people still managed to enjoy themselves. These fans at the Rainbow in London are watching a concert given by two New Wave bands – the Jam and the Clash (10, May 1977).

TRAINING AND WORK EXPERIENCE COURSES

With no guarantee of employment for school leavers, the Government initiated programmes of training and work experience courses for young people. The object was to give school leavers practical experience of working for a company or in industry, doing the type of job they might one day hope to get full-time.

> **Places would go only to those young people who had been unemployed for at least six weeks, and priority would be given to those who were the least qualified with the poorest employment prospects . . . courses . . . would . . . last for up to 12 months . . . . All young people on courses under the programme would be paid an allowance of £18 a week, including £2 for travel expenses . . .** (*Keesing's Contemporary Archives,* 1977)

Critics of the scheme claimed that it provided no real training and that the young workers were simply a form of cheap labour. How successful was this or any other work experience scheme? How do the schemes of the 1970s compare with those of today? You could ask teachers, older friends and relatives for their views. Old copies of your local newspaper may give details of work schemes that were operated in your area.

YOUNG VOTERS

In 1970 18-year-olds were allowed to vote for the first time. There was plenty of media interest in these young voters when the first by-elections of that year were held. Some new voters did not seem to know very much about party politics and decided on their choice of candidate by other means:

> **"We went to hear the Blue Man [Conservative] and the Red Man [Labour] and we couldn't make out what the Blue Man was on about. We think he fancied himself." That is how**

DRUGS

During the 1970s drug abuse became a recognized problem. The drugs most widely used were amphetamines, cannabis, L.S.D., heroin and cocaine. Many young people became addicted without realizing the dangers that drug-taking could bring. Others chose to ignore warnings such as the deaths of several rock music stars in circumstances that involved drugs. In a parliamentary debate on the Misuse of Drugs Bill (1970), the then Home Secretary, Reginald Maulding, said that with regard to the drug problem:

> **We are dealing with a symptom of a deeply troubled society. The full rigour of the law is essential. But repression alone clearly is not enough. We must identify the reasons and causes of this phenomenon. In a time like this when life should be so full of opportunity, challenge and possibility, what is the emptiness that draws so many young people towards the use of these drugs?** (*Keesing's Contemporary Archives,* June 1971)

Another contributor to the debate thought that taking drugs was just a passing craze favoured by the young, who wanted to be different from the previous generation. Do you think this is true?

Glue-sniffing was also a problem in the 1970s. Over 50 young people died as a result of solvent abuse in England and Scotland between 1970 and 1977. Why are some individuals slow to learn about the dangers of these activities? Why do they appear not to care?

> **three of Britain's first teenage voters came to decide to vote against Mr Tom King, Conservative candidate for this by-election.** (John Ezard in *The Guardian,* 12 March 1970)

What party would you vote for if you were old enough to vote in the next General Election? Why?

Law and Order

Throughout the 1970s there was concern about an increase in violence in society. The media were often blamed for projecting violent images that might influence impressionable people, especially the young. An example might be the on-the-spot T.V. coverage of scenes of violence on picket lines. Other factors held to be responsible for social unrest included racial problems, unemployment and poor living conditions. The consequences of vandalism — broken windows and doors, damaged telephone boxes, graffiti, and the destruction of purpose-built play and recreation areas — became evident in many town and city areas. Gangs of young people were often responsible for this, and also for increasing violence on the terraces at football grounds.

INDUSTRIAL DISPUTES

One of the most serious problems facing the police in the 1970s was the containment of social unrest arising from industrial disputes. One of the longest and fiercest disputes, lasting nearly 600 days, was at the Grunwick film processing company in North London. Here, low-paid Asian workers went on strike in protest at the management's refusal to negotiate with their union. The strikers claimed that they had faced:

> . . . extreme pressures from the management and the local police . . . . More serious allegations include threats and physical assault. Fifteen people have been arrested while picketing at one of the factories. The second in command [of the police] at Harlesden has strenuously denied a local M.P.'s suggestion that the police have been acting as a "company force".
> (*New Statesman*, 1 April 1977)

This is just one view of the role of the police in the dispute. How do you think they or the Home Secretary, responsible for law and order, felt about this?

SOCCER

Violence amongst football spectators caused the game's authorities to take measures to try to prevent this happening.

> **Following an invasion of their pitch by West Ham United supporters celebrating their team's 2-0 victory over Fulham in only the second all-London F.A. Cup Final this century, the Wembley authorities announced plans to erect restraining fences on part of the terracing for succeeding matches.**
> (*The Annual Register – 1975*, Longman 1976)

If there is a football league team near you, find out if it had to deal with any hooliganism during the 1970s. Does it have to deal with it today, and if so what methods has it adopted to control crowd violence?

THE POLICE NATIONAL COMPUTER

One important application of modern technology was the setting up of a police national computer. Information about criminal records and wanted and missing persons, along with vehicle owners' and drivers' details from the Department of Environment computer at Swansea, could be displayed very quickly on computer screens at police stations. Sir Robert Mark, a past Commissioner of the Metropolitan Police, describes the effectiveness of this new technology:

> **During the height of the I.R.A. bombing campaign I arrived home late one night with my wife from a police social**

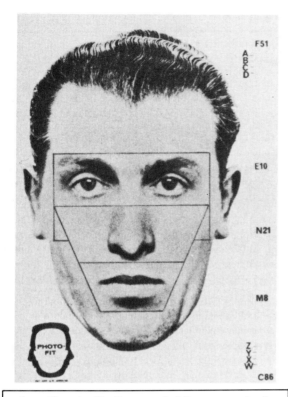

function to find my neighbours out of their homes looking with anxiety at a car parked against my garden hedge. They thought it might be a car bomb. The home beat constable from the local station arrived and was able to tell them within two minutes that it belonged to someone who lived a few hundred yards away who, for one reason or another, had decided to walk home. Before the advent of the computer and personal radio we would have cleared the area, called the Bomb Squad and it would have taken three or four hours, not two minutes, to resolve the matter. (Sir Robert Mark, *In the Office of Constable*, Collins, 1978)

Some people are concerned that so much personal information is stored on computer. Do you think the benefits computers bring to police efficiency outweigh the risks of an unauthorized person having access to the computer information?

The "Photo-Fit" identity system was adopted by the British police in April 1970. It replaced the "Identikit" system in which portraits were built up piece by piece by means of artists' sketches. "Photo-Fit" used photographs instead of sketches and the pictures produced were consequently more realistic.

THE FOURTH MAN

In 1951 two Foreign Office spies, Donald Maclean and Guy Burgess, defected to the Soviet Union. They were assisted by a then unknown "third man", later exposed as Kim Philby, who joined them in Russia. Speculation about the identity of a "fourth man" who was thought to have helped, continued until 1979 when he was named as Sir Anthony Blunt, the world-famous art historian. He was Surveyor and Adviser for the Queen's pictures and drawings, and had also been a member of the Security Service from 1940 to 1945. It was revealed that the security authorities had been aware of Blunt's spying for many years:

> ... in 1964 ... the Attorney-General ... had consented to Blunt's being offered immunity from prosecution if he confessed, in order to assist continuing investigation into the Burgess-Maclean-Philby network and Soviet penetration of the security and intelligence services and other public services. Blunt complied, admitting that he had become an agent of Russian intelligence ... and although after 1945 he was no longer in a position to supply the Russians with classified information, in 1951 he had used his old Russian contacts to help Burgess and Maclean to escape. (*Annual Register, 1979*, Longman, 1980)

Unlike some others, Blunt did not seek exile abroad when his spying became publicly known. He issued a press statement and on 20 November 1979 he gave an interview to *The Times* seeking to explain his actions. Your reference library may have copies of newspapers of the day which carried Blunt's press statement and interview.

Multi-Racial Britain

During the 1970s, when the economic recession made life more difficult, immigrant groups were blamed by some people for Britain's problems. Asians in particular became victims of racist violence. Many were intimidated or physically attacked and some had their homes set on fire. Legal moves were made to end the discrimination suffered by ethnic minorities in education, employment and housing. The Race Relations Act (1976) extended the legal prohibitions on discrimination and set up a single new Commission on Racial Equality to deal with problems.

UGANDAN ASIANS

British nationality laws gave all Commonwealth citizens the right to live in Britain, become British citizens and hold United Kingdom passports. In 1972 Idi Amin, the Ugandan President, expelled 40,000 Asians with U.K. passports from his country. The majority of them fled to Great Britain. One of these refugees, Ramijid Patel, opened a shop in Dulwich:

> When I took that shop the hours were short. I decided that if I wanted to make the business viable I must have long hours because it was a residential area. My wife and I worked 100 hours each per week. Besides that I had help from my children. That shop I kept for four years and I didn't have any holidays for four years. Refugees have nothing to lose in their life so naturally they are the hardest working people. (Quoted in P. Pagnamenta and R. Overy, *All Our Working Lives*, B.B.C., 1984)

IMMIGRANT CULTURES

Immigrant groups have brought with them a variety of skills and cultures:

> Evidence of immigrant cultures can be seen in the urban areas where most of them have settled – national dress worn by many Asian women, Indian films, Asian food shops, market stalls with West Indian fruit and vegetables – and many schools have adapted their curricula to allow host and immigrant communities better to understand each other's traditions. The needs of immigrant children for language training are being met in special centres run by the education authorities. (*Britain 1976*, H.M.S.O., 1976)

Find out to what extent the needs of immigrant children and adults were met by your local

Some people resented the Asians' success in their business ventures. Why do you think this was so?

Ugandan Asians arriving in Britain in 1972. Your local reference library may have copies of old national newspapers which will help you to find out more about the arrival and resettlement of these refugees.

amden – an equal opportunity employer

Applicants are considered on the basis of their suitability for the post regardless of sex, race and marital status. The Council also welcomes applications from disabled persons with the necessary attributes.

Following legal moves in the mid-1970s to end racial and sexual discrimination, notices like this one (Time Out, October 1979) started to appear. Today this type of notice is commonplace.

education authority in the 1970s. Your school may be able to help you contact someone who taught either at a special language centre or at a school with a large immigrant intake.

Some people thought that schools should teach immigrants to adapt to the indigenous (native) culture. Other people held the opposing view that immigrants should be helped to retain their own way of life. What are your views on this?

RACE RELATIONS

The immigrant population was concentrated in major towns and cities. Poor living conditions and economic difficulties resulting from unemployment contributed to an increase in racial tension. At times the police were criticized for discriminating against young black people:

A three-day carnival in the streets of Notting Hill, London, organized by the large West Indian community there, was used by groups of young black miscreants as an opportunity to pick pockets, loot shops, rob with threats and extort money from shopkeepers and stall-holders. Warned by previous experience, the police, who estimated there were about 800 such 'hooligans' among 150,000 'revellers', were present in force – close on 1,600 of them. Their attempts at arrests and control of crowds and traffic led to their becoming targets for stone-throwing and other assaults by the black 'hooligans', no fewer than 325 policemen being injured, 26 seriously. Black sympathizers accused the police of 'provocation' by their massive presence and argued that they should have left the Caribbean carnival alone; but the Chief Commissioner of the Metropolitan Police, Sir Robert Mark, declared: 'There are not going to be any No-Go areas in Metropolitan Police districts. The force will police every street and uphold the law.' (*Annual Register, 1976,* Longman, 1977)

★People to People Festival throughout Ealing begins on Friday, continuing until October 27. The theme is multi-racial. Events will be taking place in Acton and Southall, as well as Ealing itself, in colleges, schools, community centres, pubs and Town Halls; and will range from nationally known groups such as Banner and Broadside Theatre and MAAS Movers giving performances, through to a concert by local schoolchildren. There will be jazz and Irish Folk evenings, photographic exhibitions, a Rock Against Racism concert, a children's day, Street Theatre and a cabaret evening. Tickets and further information from ECRC 2, The Green, High St, Ealing, W5 (579 3861).

★Asian Day in Balham A day of music, dance, drama, food and costume from India, Pakistan and Bangladesh. On Saturday, during the afternoon and evening. For further information, contact Nick Wright at WCCR, 172 Lavender Hill, SW11 (228 8032). Admission free.

Advertisements for multi-cultural events in the late 1970s. Other well-known festivals brought to Britain by immigrant groups include the Notting Hill Carnival and Chinese New Year celebrations, both in London.

Efforts were made to improve relations between the police and immigrants. The police tried to encourage more recruits from ethnic minorities, and officers were made aware of the need to learn about different cultures. Immigrant leaders were consulted about the policing of community events. Are relations between the police and immigrant communities more harmonious today?

The Changing Role of Women

Many women began to challenge the assumption that their main roles in life were those of housewife and mother. They wanted to be treated as equals to men in law, in employment and in pay. The 1970 Equal Pay Act and the 1975 Sex Discrimination Act were passed by parliament to remedy the situation. These new laws helped to protect women from discrimination but the attitudes of society needed to change before there could be real equality. Some forms of language were altered to avoid discrimination. The new title "Ms" began to be used instead of Miss or Mrs which revealed a women's married status. Feminists also preferred terms like "chairperson" and "spokesperson" to chairman and spokesman with their male connotations.

WOMEN IN MEN'S JOBS

Some psychologists in the 1970s claimed that job sex-stereotyping began as early as at the age of ten. Girls were persuaded to think of becoming nurses, secretaries or receptionists and dissuaded by parents and careers advisers from wanting to be engineers, bricklayers or bulldozer operators. An article in *Ideal Home* (November 1979) describes the problems experienced by two women in male-dominated occupations. The first, a female carpenter, answered a council's advertisement for carpenters:

> **The council's first reaction was to say they were waiting for their cost cuts to be announced before employing more carpenters. It wasn't until Rene posed the 64,000-dollar question: "It's not because I'm a woman is it?" that things started moving; a job was found for her almost immediately.**

When the second girl applied to become a gas service engineer:

> **... there was some apprehension about her strength and stamina, but as Anne points out, some of her male colleagues are smaller than her own 5ft 2in [1.73m]. Lifting heavy heaters and cookers is not a problem as they're taught how to lift those at the outset.**

In your opinion, are there any occupations which are more suited to men than women or vice versa? What are the reasons for your answers?

SEX DISCRIMINATION

After the 1975 Sex Discrimination Act it was illegal to advertize – with a few exceptions – for specific male or female employees. Before this act, adverts like the following appeared regularly in newspapers and magazines:

> **Eminent divorce lawyers need well-groomed young lady able to represent at court occasionally.**

> **Attractive girl required to be receptionist on show stand at Paris Air Show.** (*The Times*, 10 March 1971)

Find some post-1975 adverts to compare with the above. Look for terms such as "salesperson" and "bar person".

The 1970s saw the opening of many women's centres – some funded by council grants – and the staging of other events exclusively by women for women.

★**The Sex Discrimination Act and How to Use It** One-day study conference, 17 November, organised by Rights of Women to help women understand and use the Act. At the Architectural Association, Bedford Square, WC1. Fee £2, unwaged 75p.

★**Haringey Women's Centre Opening Party** With poetry reading by women from 'One Foot Off the Mountain' at 8.00 and feminist sing-song at 9.30. Bring food and booze to share. Starts 7.00 at 40 Turnpike Lane, N8.

★**The Women's Arts Alliance** 10 Cambridge Terrace Mews, off Chester Gate, Regents Park, NW1 (935 1841); are offering a variety of courses, beginning this month and next. Subjects include Tai Chi, Self Defence, Life Drawing, Karate, Electric Guitar, Piano, Feminist Psychics, 'Woman Dance' and Body Language Awareness.

"HAVE THINGS GONE TOO FAR?"

The following letter appeared in *The Guardian* on 10 May 1979, seven days after Margaret Thatcher had become Britain's first woman Prime Minister:

Sir,
Have things gone too far? My sovereign is a woman; my Prime Minister is a woman; my boss is a woman; and my wife is a woman.
Yours faithfully,
C. Grimwood.

For some women though, things had not progressed:

Today there are still girls who grow up believing that the biggest events of their lives will be getting married and having children; they see employment as a kind of stop-gap between leaving school and finding true happiness with Mr Right. (Anna Coote, *Equal at Work? Women in Men's Jobs*, Collins, 1979)

Ask older female friends or relatives if they were influenced by the feminist movement in the 1970s and whether their expectations of life changed.

In 1977 the London Borough of Camden made history by appointing Claudine Eccleston as their first woman plumber.

MARGARET THATCHER

Margaret Thatcher's political stance and tough talking led the Russians to nickname her "The Iron Lady". Christopher Booker wrote that some people thought she might bring a female influence to bear on the running of national affairs. This failed to happen, in his opinion, for the following reasons:

What people who held this view failed to grasp was the simple psychological truth that women who get on in politics do so because it is the "male" element in them which is hyperactive . . . . Mrs Thatcher's driving force throughout her career has always been that masculine element in her which led her to become a lawyer and an industrial chemist, which gave her such a careful, legalistic mind and her habit of always seeming, even in the most friendly interview, to be straining to make some over-insistent, contrary point. (Christopher Booker, *The Seventies, Portrait of a Decade*, Allen Lane, 1980)

Do you agree with Christopher Booker's assumption that men and women have different personal characteristics? Ask friends of the opposite sex for their opinion.

Housing and Buildings

Some developments in housing in the 1970s were more successful than others. The tower blocks of the 1960s were considered a failure and urban redevelopment schemes met opposition from groups wishing to preserve old areas. New high technology industries moved to purpose-built premises on the edge of new or expanding towns. The employment these industries offered persuaded many people to settle in new towns such as Telford and Milton Keynes. There was concern about the social problems of inner-city life. Poor housing and shabby environments were two factors contributing to the unrest which culminated in the riots of the early 1980s in London, Liverpool and Bristol.

HIGH-RISE TOWER BLOCKS

During the 1970s high-rise buildings went out of fashion. It was finally realized, at great financial and social cost, that:

> ... **this was not the way most people chose to live, or could live without grievous social damage. In 1972 the Department of the Environment produced a survey on high-rise blocks which revealed a large majority of mothers as being dissatisfied with play provision. It must have been an understatement .... Adventure playgrounds sprang up on waste ground ... and they filled a want. But some children preferred to find their own adventures, plan their own assaults. There was a period when the new tower blocks were getting broken even before they were occupied. The social damage was worse. Perpendicular living aggravated a process already advanced in our urban life, the decline of neighbourliness.** (Norman Shrapnel, *The Seventies – Britain's Inward March*, Constable, 1980)

Many blocks were demolished only 20 or 30 years after being built. Find out if your local authority made regulations about the height of any new tower blocks built in the early 1970s.

NEW TOWNS

The decay of many inner cities and an increase in the population made the provision of more homes necessary. One way of doing this was to build complete new towns with all the housing, industry, roads, and leisure facilities planned from the beginning. Christopher Booker wrote about his visit to Milton Keynes in the early 1970s:

> **All is still remote rural peace, on the site of what in three years' time is destined to be "the largest City Centre complex in Europe", a mile long and half-a-mile wide. On nearby hilltops stand the first housing estates of a new city ... hundreds of grim little misshapen boxes, in brick or corrugated metal, turned out by machine.** (Christopher Booker, *The Seventies, Portrait of a Decade*, Allen Lane, 1980)

You could write to the main library or Council Offices of a new town to find out more about its development. Other useful sources of information are the Development Corporations which help to run new towns. Your reference library will help you to find the necessary addresses.

Many provincial theatres were built during the 1970s. This theatre and library complex was opened in Bromley, Kent in 1977.

RENOVATING OLD PROPERTIES

Householders could obtain Renovation Grants for providing amenities such as bathrooms, for modernizing homes and for converting large properties into flats. In Ironbridge the local Development Corporation restored many old properties as an example to individuals who might be considering their own improvements:

> **Tiny cottages and sizeable houses are among the interesting old properties that are being carefully restored for sale on the open market . . . . We want to encourage people who may be considering buying old properties and doing the restoration work themselves. It is not always realized that there are various grants available for this type of work.** (*Ideal Home*, November 1979)

Find out about the grants that were available in your area in the 1970s, by asking at your Town Hall or Council Offices.

SECOND HOMES

For those who could afford them, second homes, especially country cottages, became very fashionable. An article in *Punch* gives us this picture of a family and their weekend cottage:

> **Every weekend . . . they beetle down to the cottage – a beamed, low-ceilinged job, with a stone floor, wide yawning fireplace (a must, a must) and an unkempt Amazonian garden for the children to vanish into . . . . However comfortably [the owner] lives in his blonde-furnitured, eye-level-grilled and water-bedded home in London, here he and his family unit seem willing to put up with the kind of discomfort that peasant farmers revolted over at the height of the Agricultural Revolution.** (*Punch*, 8 August 1973)

In what way does the writer poke fun at those with country cottages?

Transport

Two factors particularly influenced developments in transport during the 1970s. One was the energy crisis and the consequent need to save oil. The other was a growing awareness of the need to protect the environment from pollution. Some towns and cities tried to reduce traffic on their roads by introducing "park and ride" schemes whereby drivers left their cars either at home or just outside the city centre and used public transport instead. Walking, jogging or cycling to work became fashionable not just with keep-fit enthusiasts but also with people trying to save fuel and reduce pollution.

CONCORDE

In November 1977 Concorde, the world's first supersonic passenger airliner, finally flew from London to New York after months of protest from Americans worried about noise and vibration levels. Earlier in the 1970s British people living near the test routes had also been concerned about the effect of "sonic booms" on people, animals and buildings. Laurie Lee flew on Concorde and described what happened when they passed the speed of sound:

> **I stood and braced myself. We were still climbing steeply. The needle moved from 0.94 to Mach 1. I was standing facing the dials. It felt as though someone had lightly brushed against me. We had passed the speed of sound. "Mach One-plus", someone said. The big needle stood steady, but some of the other dials seemed suddenly to go crazy: pointers see-sawed, swung; numbers raced and clicked, indicators jerked and hiccoughed. Nothing else appeared to happen. The crew went on with their figures. So that was that.**
> (Laurie Lee, *I Can't Stay Long*, André Deutsch, 1975)

Many different views are held about Concorde. Some people admire its design and appearance. Other people think it is an expensive "white elephant". What are your feelings about it? Do you know how fast the speed of sound is?

Private Eye's satirical comment on the number of passengers on Concorde's inaugural flight.

JUMBO JETS

Boeing 747 aircraft, or "jumbo jets", began their first regular passenger flights in the early 1970s and soon became one of the most common airliners in use. They differed from the conventional narrow aircraft in size and in their more spacious internal arrangements.

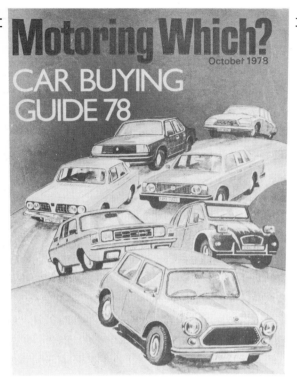

Motoring Which?

October 1978

CAR BUYING GUIDE 78

You can learn about the shape and design of 1970s cars from magazine photographs or cover illustrations such as this one. Which letters were used as part of the registration number to date 1970s vehicles?

HIGH SPEED TRAINS

British Rail's new 125 m.p.h. high speed train came into operation in late 1976. Its introduction made inter-city transport quicker and more attractive for commuters and business people. The following extract from *The Guardian* describes a V.I.P. trip arranged for journalists and television men:

The high speed train ... bore him [the

The sheer size of a jumbo jet never ceases to surprise. It seems inconceivable that it will ever get off the ground. It is 230 feet [70m] long with a span of 195 feet [59.5m]. It has seating for 27 first class and 335 economy class passengers. (Des Wilson, *The Illustrated London News*, May 1975)

CYCLING

The environmental pressure group Friends of the Earth launched a campaign in 1975 to promote cycling and make it safe. Their supporters' newspaper describes how this campaign

... got off to a flying start in 1975 with 3000 cyclists taking part in one of the biggest rides in 20 years. Pressure from Friends of the Earth forced the Government to accept a FoE amendment to the Transport Bill giving local authorities the power to provide cycle parking facilities. Indeed cycle use grew rapidly in the 1970s, and FoE's 1979 Reclaim the Road Rally filled Trafalgar Square with 6000 cyclists.

What facilities are there in your area for cycle parking? What other measures have been taken to help cyclists?

Guardian **correspondent] to Paddington in 48 minutes (from Swindon) which was two minutes ahead of schedule and 18 minutes faster than an ordinary express. Officials on board were anxious to say how fast the entire journey had been, and how very comfortable with wall-to-wall carpeting, air-cushioned disc-braked bogies, ergonomic seats, double glazing, automatic doors and Lord knows what else.** (Dennis Johnson in *The Guardian* 1 May 1976)

A faster rail service meant that more people could commute long distances to work. Why do some people prefer commuting by rail rather than driving to work? What is the fastest speed that a British Rail passenger train is capable of today?

Medical Progress

Many advances in medical science were made possible by the use of new technology. Developments in lasers and computers enabled doctors to perform surgery and to diagnose complaints in ways which had not previously been possible. The birth of the first test-tube baby brought new hope for childless couples. Ultrasound scans using high-frequency sound waves enabled doctors and parents to see images of an unborn baby inside its mother's uterus. Natural medicine became very popular. Naturopaths, osteopaths, homeopaths, medical herbalists and acupuncturists were consulted by many people looking for an alternative form of treatment.

THE FIRST TEST-TUBE BABY

The world's first test-tube baby, Louise Brown, was born on 25 July 1978, in Oldham, Lancashire. It had been thought that her mother would be unable to have children because of a blockage in her fallopian tubes. But two British doctors, Patrick Steptoe and Robert Edwards, pioneered a method whereby a female egg cell could be removed from a woman, fertilized by the husband's sperm in a laboratory and then replaced in the woman's uterus. The birth of Louise was the culmination of more than ten years of research by the two doctors. Questions were raised, however, about this method of fertilization:

> In common with most major steps in medical sciences, and particularly those emerging from research in reproductive biology, the latest advance raises moral questions of great social importance . . . . The long-term issue raised by the birth is to question what this development means for the genetic engineer. It is one thing to help a childless couple to conceive by overcoming an obstacle to conception, even a major one. It would be another to create new interferences with the process of life. (*The Times*, 27 July 1978)

Why were some people worried that abuse of the technology which had produced the first test-tube baby might take place?

LASERS

Laser is short for Light Amplification by the Stimulated Emission of Radiation. It is a device which produces beams of a special kind of light. Medical lasers were used mainly to seal blood vessels cut in operations, weld detached eye retinas back into place and to destroy growths. Operations using lasers came to be called "bloodless surgery". In 1978 a new laser treatment for the early stages of cervical cancer was successfully carried out in Birmingham:

> Until now . . . treatment has involved minor surgery and several days in hospital . . . . [Now] if trouble is found it can be treated with the laser as a simple out-patient procedure, painlessly and without any anaesthetic.

The doctor in charge of the work hoped that

> . . . each major centre in the country will eventually have its own laser and a team trained to use it. In this way we can not only cure but also avoid the necessity for more radical and more expensive in-patient care. We estimate that in our first five out-patient sessions we saved the NHS [National Health Service] some £7000. (Wendy Cooper in *The Guardian*, 12 July 1978)

Find out if your nearest hospital performed laser treatment in the 1970s.

BODY SCANNERS

The 1979 Nobel Prize in physiology or medicine was won by an Englishman, Dr Godfrey Hounsfield, for the development of a whole body X-ray scanner. His C.A.T. (computer-assisted tomography) scanner was one of the most important innovations in medical technology in the 1970s. This extract explains how it worked:

> ... the body scanner took larger numbers of low-dosage pictures from different angles, processed the results in a computer, and fed them out as detailed three-dimensional pictures of organs such as the lungs, pancreas, kidneys and other internal structures "seen" from any required angle. Beside being three-dimensional, these pictures were far clearer and more detailed than those taken either with conventional X-ray machines or by any other means.
> (*Annual Register, 1975*, Longman, 1976)

The clarity of the pictures was especially useful in finding deep-lying tumours and in establishing their shape and size with great precision.

HEALTHY LIVING

Exercise and a balanced diet were recommended for those wishing to avoid heart disease. Certain foods were considered particularly beneficial:

> ... pulses (beans and peas), most whole grains (wheat, buckwheat, millet, oats, barley, rye), potassium-rich fruits such as grapes and peaches, and certain vegetables – notably onions and garlic. If these are included in a balanced diet which also avoids meat, animal fat (dairy products), refined sugar and refined flour, and reduces salt intake, then the nutritional needs of the individual will be met and heart-disease causative factors reduced. (*Here's Health*, July 1979)

Littlehampton
The Peoples Medical Supplies, 14 Bayford Road, Littlehampton, BN17 5HL (opposite GPO). Tel: Littlehampton 6706.

Llandeilo
Regency Health Shop, 109 Rhosmaen Street, Llandeilo, Dyfed. Tel: 3556. Also Osteopathic treatment.

Llanelli, Dyfed
Jelfs Health & Herbal Stores, 17 Central Precinct, Llanelli, Dyfed. Dried Herbs, Herbal Remedies, Vitamins, Biochemic Remedies, Books, Cosmetics, Wholemeal Bread.

London
E12, Barkers Health Store, 690 Romford Road, Manor Park. E12. Tel: 01-514 2800.
EC3, Health & Beauty Centre, 9 Tower Hill Place (opposite Tower of London). Tel: 01-626 0261. Specialists in natural vitamins, herbal remedies, homoeopathy, cosmetics, nature cure.
N22, Minton, 5 High Road, Wood Green, (Turnpike Lane Underground). Healthfood Store. efficient, Friendly, Unhurried Service. 9-7 weekdays, Saturdays 9-6), Tel: 01-888 4289. Now also at this address, Health & Beauty Foodstore, 42 High Street, Southgate, London N14. Tel: 886 1990.
NW7, Healthways, Broadway, Mill Hill. An independent healthstore offering friendly service. Tel: 01-959 0771.
W13, West Ealing Health Food, Yoga & Slimming Centre, 3 Leeland Road. Large range of remedies, Wholefoods, Organic and Natural Honeys, Free range Eggs, Organic Vegetables. Qualified Herbalist, Osteopath, Acupuncturist and Reflexologist in attendance. Quick Slim Herbal Slimming Wrap – 1½ hour sessions. Family Business. Tel: 01-567 4638.
W14, Westken Wholefoods, 6 Charleville Road. Open 9.00-6.30 Mon-Sat. Full range of health foods also bulk supplies at reduced prices. Please ring for details 01-385 0956.

An increased interest in healthy living resulted in the opening of many health food shops. Here is part of a directory of health foodstores printed in Here's Health *magazine (July 1979).*

Look in copies of natural health magazines from the 1970s for their advice about diet and exercise. (Examples include *Health Now, Healthy Living* and *Yoga Today*.) If there is a health food shop near you ask them which health foods are popular now.

Everyday Technology

By the end of the 1970s there were many situations in everyday life that brought people into contact with computers. Cash dispensers, computer games and learning programmes, word processors, computerized library tickets and supermarket checkouts are just some illustrations of how the computer revolutionized life. The discovery in 1971 that it was possible to place all the main electronic parts of a computer on one tiny silicon chip enabled small, relatively cheap micro-computers to be built. By the late 1970s these were to be found in many schools, homes and small businesses. This process culminated in 1980 with the ZX80, the first home computer selling for under £100, brought out by Clive Sinclair.

VIDEO RECORDERS

The first home video machines appeared in the early 1970s. They used one-hour tapes and had very simple controls. In the beginning they were far too expensive for the majority of people to purchase.

> **Anyone with cash to spare for a piece of status-bolstering gadgetry in a luxury class beyond the reach of most can now buy himself a Philips home video recorder for £275 . . .** (*The Times*, 26 January 1970)

Two years later the following article appeared in *The Listener*:

> **All that the video-cassette machine will do for the viewer is release him from the necessity of watching a programme at the time it is transmitted (if the machine is fitted with its own tuner, he could record a programme on one channel while watching another), and of course he could repeat a programme until tired of it . . . . When there is a sufficient number of players in existence I would expect to see pre-recorded tapes coming onto the market, but the real effort at mass distribution of video programmes will not come until a low cost replay-only system reaches the market.** (*The Listener*, 8 June 1972)

POCKET CALCULATORS

Clive Sinclair brought out the world's first pocket calculator in 1972. It sold for £79 and helped to make Sinclair a household name. Robin Edmunds recalls his first sight of one of these new gadgets:

> **It was about 8 by 4 inches in size and had approximately 16 metal pads marked with numbers and mathematical symbols built onto the surface of one side. There was a metal "pencil" attached by a wire at the side of the gadget, an on/off switch and a display unit at the top covered in clear perspex. Fascinated, I watched my friend solve a complicated problem with this gadget. He used the pencil to tap out a series of numbers on the metal pads. Within seconds the answer appeared in the display unit.** (Robin Edmunds, born in 1952.)

How do the pocket calculators of today compare in size, appearance and price? Ask any older friends or relatives if they have similar memories to the one described above.

How do the features of modern video recorders compare with those of the original machines, listed above? Was the article correct in predicting the arrival of a replay-only system?

"Wait! Which one of us is going to let the videotape machine slip out in casual conversation?"

A cartoon from Punch *(30 May 1979) illustrating how early video recorders were considered to be status symbols.*

COMPUTERS IN THE LIBRARY

Bromley was one of the first London boroughs to change to a computerized system of issuing library books. Previously readers had individual card tickets which they exchanged for books. The following extract explains the new system.

> **Each reader has his own bright orange ticket, and each book has a white ticket, with its own identifying marks. When a reader wishes to borrow a book, the librarian inserts both tickets in two slots and identification of the book and the reader is registered on tape. This reel is later fed into the computer where the data is processed. The library staff can then check when any book was borrowed, and by whom.** (The *Bromley Times*, 6 November 1970)

Does your library have a computer? Ask the librarian how it works.

COMPUTERS AND PERSONAL INFORMATION

As computers became more widely used there was concern about the amount and type of personal information that could be stored in them. A Committee on Privacy was set up in May 1970 to look into the possible invasion of privacy that might arise from the use of computers. The committee recommended that:

> **Legislation should be introduced to provide for the setting up of a standard commission to keep under review the growth of techniques of gathering and handling personal information by computer . . . . Each business firm should at once, on a voluntary basis, both adopt a code of practice for handling personal information, and the concept of appointing "a responsible person" from among staff concerning the handling of computerized personal information.** (*Whitaker's Almanack*, 1973)

Who, in your opinion, should have the right to store personal information on computer, and who should be allowed access to it?

Sport and Leisure

Some new sports appeared in the 1970s. Jogging began as a craze but soon became an important part of the regular exercise taken by a large number of people. Hang-gliding offered excitement and danger. Yoga was regarded with suspicion by some people as part of the "hippy" movement and a fashion that would soon die out. However it has since become an established leisure activity. Revolutionary changes came to the traditional world of cricket with the wearing of extra protective clothing by batsmen facing fast bowlers, and with the establishment of Kerry Packer's series of alternative matches. Violent rioting by English soccer fans in Europe in 1975 led to the coining of the phrase "The English Disease" by *F.I.F.A. News*, organ of the International Football Federation.

JOGGING

In a magazine article, the Labour politician Roy Hattersley described his enthusiasm for jogging.

Of course, it is still an effort to start and a relief to finish. But once I have forced myself over the first few yards real enjoyment sets in, and there is a special satisfaction in lying back, submerged in hot water and the knowledge that I ran again today. I still pant when I walk upstairs or pick up small parcels. But I can run for two uninterrupted miles. And on good days with the wind behind me I sometimes manage three. (Roy Hattersley in the *New Statesman*, 31 March 1978)

Do you know anyone who took up jogging in the 1970s? Ask them why they started.

For more serious runners there were half and full marathons to compete in. Others preferred fun runs such as this Evening Standard *"Jog-in" which took place in 1978.*

HANG-GLIDING

You stand at the edge of the hill, waiting nervously for the wind to be just right. Then, three or four rapid strides, and you are swept off your feet as if by a chair-lift. The hang-glider is airborne, and you are suspended: the ground has suddenly dropped away and is now 200 ft below. Your only concern is to control the glider: your life depends on it. (Roland Adburgham in the *Sunday Times Magazine*, 9 July 1978)

Some serious injuries and a few deaths resulted from crashes, forcing the British Hang Gliding Association to tighten up the sport's regulations. This did not stop enthusiasts from taking off from any available hill, and one motorized hang-glider even flew the English Channel.

YOGA

Yoga is an activity that relaxes the body and the mind through a combination of slow stretching exercises and meditation. Here are Avril Harrild's memories of her yoga classes in the early 1970s.

There were no sports or leisure centres in Bromley where I lived so yoga classes were started in halls or large rooms. Leotards and tracksuits were not the fashion then so I went dressed in comfortable trousers and a top. We were extremely squashed in the room. The headstand that one associated with yoga was never attempted at this class because the tutor felt it was too dangerous with so many people in the room. The squat position I remember well as we were encouraged to use this

CRICKET

An Australian named Kerry Packer used financial inducements to persuade many of the world's top players, including England's captain, Tony Greig, to leave their national teams and to play for him instead. His Super-World Series of matches, all staged in Australia, were promoted and televised in a way that had more in common with show-business than the traditional world of cricket.

Packer's plans have caused a deep and maybe incurable schism in the game. Now after nearly seven months of talking and an investment of several million pounds, his so-called cricket circus is about to become a fact. The traditional cricket world has already been shattered and Packer himself has been roundly condemned. He has shown though that he is ruthlessly determined to succeed, he has a record of success behind him and it would be naive to assume his plans for cricket are bound to fail. (Henry Blofeld, *The Guardian*, 23 November 1977)

Find out if Kerry Packer's World Series matches were successful and if they had any long-term effects on the game of cricket.

position whenever we felt tired or fraught. The class always finished with ten minutes relaxation. I cannot remember the name given to the type of yoga that we did but our tutor had learnt the art whilst serving in the Far East with the army during the Second World War. (Avril Harrild, born in 1942)

New Crazes

There were many crazes that emerged in the 1970s. Some of them began in the United States and were soon taken up by the rest of the western world. What are the crazes of today? How does word spread about a new craze?

SKATEBOARDING

Skateboarding was keenly enjoyed by many young people in the 1970s. A skateboard is a long, shaped board set on wheels which can carry its rider along at great speed. Protective clothing – helmets, gloves, elbow and knee pads – have to be worn by the skateboarders. Because of the dangers of skateboarding in the streets some local authorities and business people set up special parks with ramps and other obstacles for the skateboarders to negotiate. Not everyone was keen on the idea of these parks.

A huge outcry has erupted against the plan to build a deluxe skatepark in Bromley's Library Gardens.

Skateboarders have welcomed the scheme but many local residents are up in arms and one is already organizing a petition. Residents believe the park would bring extra noise and traffic to the residential area. (The *Bromley Times*, 5 January 1978)

Do you still see young people skateboarding today? Is there a special skateboard park in your area? If so, find out when it was built and if there was any local opposition to it.

A cartoon showing how popular skateboards were with young people.

"Right—off skateboards everybody"

STREAKING

Streaking means running naked in a public place. In the 1970s streakers ran across bridges in London and interrupted rugby and cricket matches. Various explanations for this craze were suggested.

> **The new fad, popularly known as "streaking" has been observed with various shades of amusement and disgust . . . [it] has come to be regarded as a dare, a means for displaying courage in defiance of conventional mores, or just "fun". Events will show whether it passes on the way fashions demand; whether it persists as an expression of anxiety or hostility, or whether it is a precursor [forerunner] of renewed direct action.** (*New Society*, 21 March 1974)

MARTIAL ARTS

Martial arts films made in Hong Kong were released in Britain in the late 1960s and early 1970s. Most of them had simple revenge plots which were a vehicle for the display of oriental unarmed combat techniques. In 1972 these films became box-office smash hits in Britain and the term "Kung Fu" (one of the martial arts) became widely known and used. Another result of these films was the demand for martial arts instruction. By 1977 the interest had grown to the extent that the Government and Sports Council recognized the Martial Arts Commission as the official controlling body of the martial arts and granted it financial aid. Mr Denis Howell, the Minister for Sport, noted that

> **. . . over the past few years there has been a rapidly growing interest in the martial arts . . . . There has been financial exploitation of the public due to the high demand for instructors. It is . . . important that the martial arts are taught in a highly disciplined and**

The "unisex" look, where both men and women dressed in similar clothes, was a fashion craze at the beginning of the decade. These notices were to be seen at the Young Vic Theatre when it opened in London in 1970.

BIO-RHYTHMS

For a short while many people were interested in how bio-rhythms could govern their lives.

> **I've been looking into bio-rhythms, the latest craze. The idea is that your life, from birth to death, is governed by three rhythms: physical . . . emotional . . . and intellectual . . . . There is an active period when you discharge energy, and a passive period when you recharge it. The point at which you pass from one to the other is a critical day . . . . A double critical day, with two rhythms crossing, is worse. Once a year you have a treble critical day, and the best thing you can do is stay in bed with the blankets over your head.** (Mervyn Jones in the *New Statesman*, 1 April 1977)

People were able to buy a chart which showed their personal rhythms and advised them how to plan their lives accordingly. Why do you think the idea appealed to so many people?

> **responsible manner. Otherwise there is a risk of their becoming an excuse for violent and anti-social activities.** (*The Times*, 6 August 1977)

Was there any martial arts instruction available in your area in the 1970s? How much interest is there in the martial arts today?

Fashionable Living

A total look, either for individuals or their homes, became very popular in the 1970s. The Biba boutique, Laura Ashley and Habitat are all examples of stores which offered a complete look to the shopper. A revolt against nicely co-ordinated fashion styles came with the first hearing of "punk" music. Popular music had always influenced fashion and crazes for young people. Now coloured, spiked hair, chains, safety-pins and torn clothes became the uniform of the young punk fan. Jeans were still worn by many young people and became a more acceptable fashion for older people.

LAURA ASHLEY

As more people hoped to escape the present for what seemed a more romantic past, Laura Ashley's flower-printed dresses of calico, cotton and lace seemed the ideal accompaniment to the back-to-nature lifestyle that some people were seeking. An article in *The Times*, "Growing Organic Clothes", describes a typical Laura Ashley customer:

> **Her clothes possess precisely the qualities demanded by a certain sort of customer who might once have been considered a bit strange and arty crafty but is now recognized [as the] mainstream in fashion. Ashley clothes fit in with hypo-allergic [i.e. more natural] cosmetics, milk face washes, ethnic dress, conservation and home grown food and there is no reason why they should go out of style any faster than the ideas they seem to complement so well.** (*The Times*, 22 August 1972)

Ask older friends and relatives if they have any Laura Ashley clothes or fabrics from the 1970s.

Ethnic styles of clothing became popular in the mid-1970s. Peru, India, Morocco and Russia were some of the countries that influenced this colourful peasant-style look.

THE PUNK LOOK

From about 1976, punk music and clothes became popular with many young people. An article in *The Guardian* about punk rock contained this description of some of the music's fans:

> **... strings of multi-coloured razor blades dangle from ears; large safety pins apparently stuck through noses ... girls making up their eyes with elongated mascaraed feline flourishes and bunching up side-tufts of hair into cat's ears, while dyeing the close-cropped centre a different colour.** (John Cunningham, *The Guardian*, 16 July 1977)

Punks often used food-dye as a quick and cheap means of colouring their hair. Other elements of punk style were T-shirts carrying aggressive slogans and clothes made from plastic bin-liners.

Examples of Habitat furniture from 1977.

HABITAT

Habitat started with one store in 1964 but became an extremely fashionable place to shop in the 1970s when Terence Conran opened many more stores nationwide. With its simple, modern, well-designed and moderately priced furniture and houseware, Habitat changed the look of many of our homes.

Habitat merchandise is not just a collection of nice-looking things . . . . The products, the look of the shops and the general atmosphere, reflect a certain attitude to life and a way of living. Conran says "If you go into a shop with a mishmash of styles . . . you confuse the customer . . . there is no feeling that 'This is our style, like it or leave it'. Our confidence and style are convincing to people who shop with us." (Barty Phillips, *Conran and the Habitat Story*, Weidenfeld and Nicolson, 1984)

Habitat designs were originally aimed at young upmarket buyers. If you have a Habitat store near you, see if this is still the case. Do you think Habitat has influenced other shops in the design of furniture, glass, pottery, etc?

SEVENTIES SNAPSHOTS

Keith Waterhouse, the journalist and writer, provides us with an insight into the decade with the following written "snapshots" of people in the 1970s:

They had identical phone-in accents, grew identical mature-student beards or frizzed their hair in the same golliwog perms, wore the same type of sneakers and the same, or same looking denim shreds and patches.

An off-duty punk rocker wearing a save-the-whale T-shirt and Levis. But with green hair.

Audio typists wearing high-protein fun jewellery (a hamburger, a half-eaten doughnut) in the queue for a health-bar grated-cheese salad. (Keith Waterhouse, *Waterhouse at Large*, Michael Joseph, 1985)

Look through old magazines and family albums for photographic snapshots of people in the 1970s.

Popular Entertainment

Many disaster films were made in the 1970s and later went on to become box-office smash hits. Science fiction retained its appeal, with *Star Wars* becoming the cult film of the late 1970s. Many films were lavish productions, unmatched by T.V., aiming to get audiences back into the cinema. Another way of attracting more people was for old large cinemas to be converted into three smaller ones, each showing a different film. A craze for disco music started with the film *Saturday Night Fever*, starring John Travolta. An alternative to the disco sound was New Wave punk bands who wanted to restore a live, raw sound to the music world. More established stars, such as Elvis Presley, retained their popularity. His death in 1978 was mourned by millions worldwide.

MONTY PYTHON

One of the most inventive and irreverent T.V. comedy programmes to be broadcast during the 1970s was *Monty Python's Flying Circus*. The B.B.C. broadcast four series between October 1969 and December 1974 and during that time the programme attracted a large cult following, especially among young people.

> **The programmes were very different from any other comedy shows that I had seen. The sketches could be described as silly, absured or brilliant depending on your viewpoint. For example, often the cast wouldn't finish a sketch with a conventional punchline. Instead someone would come on and stop the sketch because "It was too silly" or a policeman would appear and arrest the cast. One of their most famous sketches was "The Ministry of Silly Walks" performed by John Cleese and Michael Palin. It was about a man trying to obtain a government grant for his silly walk. John Cleese's silly walk is still one of the funniest things that I have seen on TV.** (Pamela Harper, born 1952)

Why, do you think, did this particular series meet with such mixed reactions?

JAWS

Jaws is a film about a great white shark which marauds the coast of a thriving American sea-side resort. The following extract describes why the film was so successful. When the article was written the film was already an all-time box-office record-maker.

> **The story accords very happily with demonstrable current box-office tastes: a revived yearning for traditional action adventure, and the odd phenomenon that in a period of acute anxiety ... audiences apparently yearn for vicarious [substituted] experiences of fictional disaster.** (*The Times*, 17 December 1975)

Look in old copies of your local newspaper to see if cinema attendances broke any records when *Jaws* was showing in your area.

WATERSHIP DOWN

One of the best selling books of the 1970s was *Watership Down* by Richard Adams, about a group of rabbits escaping from their home, which is going to be bulldozed for a new housing development, and their adventures as they try to establish a new warren. The book was seen by many not just as a fantasy adventure about rabbits, but as a story of the animals' struggles to survive in man's technological world.

One of the most popular singers of the 1970s was David Bowie. Many young people copied his style of face make-up as shown on the cover of his L.P. Aladdin Sane.

It is no accident that men with their cars, trains, bulldozers, traps and gassing devices, are by and large seen in the book as "enemies".... Equally it is no accident that ... the rabbits' adventure is set in motion in the first place as an attempt to escape from that supreme symbol of the steady advance of an alien, dehumanizing future – a development scheme – nor at a deeper level still that the whole book should be about an attempt to escape from the man-made horrors into some place of distant, happy, innocent security. (Christopher Booker, *The Seventies, Portrait of a Decade*, Allen Lane, 1980)

Borrow a copy of *Watership Down* from the library. Do you agree with Christopher Booker's assessment of the story?

POPULAR MUSIC

The following extract describes the punk sound that burst onto the pop music scene in the mid-1970s:

The punks are busy ranting, spitting and vomiting their way to the top .... The adrenalin-fuelled "new wave" sound, a relentless high speed mix of almost clockwork drumming, robotic guitar chords, and screamed vocals represents a revolt against the over-sophisticated excesses of "studio" rock: punk rock was meant to be as live as a high voltage socket, unrehearsed, if necessary badly mixed, but vibrant with the unrestrained energy and violence of the street. (*The Listener*, 30 June 1977)

A complete contrast to the punk style can be seen in one of the most popular peace songs of the early 1970s, "Imagine", written and performed by John Lennon, one of the Beatles. Here is part of the song:

Imagine there's no heaven
It's easy if you try
No hell below us
Above us only sky
Imagine all the people
Living for today ....

Imagine there's no countries
It isn't hard to do
Nothing to kill or die for
And no religion too
Imagine all the people
Living life in peace ....

Borrow a copy of this record and some punk music from your library. Which do you prefer?

Holidays

The 1970s began with an increasing number of British people taking holidays abroad. A foreign holiday, along with owning a car and and T.V., became an expected part of life for many people. Britain became less than half an hour from the Continent, with regular hovercraft crossings of the English Channel.

Many passengers enjoyed day-trips shopping in the French hypermarkets. Cheap package tours brought Europe within the reach of many people's pockets, and the low fares of Laker Airways made the United States more accessible.

PACKAGE HOLIDAYS

By the early 1970s the package tour, usually to a Mediterranean resort, had become the most popular form of holiday. The flight, the accommodation, the meals, and sometimes even the entertainment were included in the cost, which was now within the price range of many people other than a wealthy few. Unfortunately some package tours did not live up to the expectations of the holidaymakers:

> My first taste of a foreign holiday was a package tour to Rimini, Italy in 1972. The night flight was straightforward but we arrived at our hotel only to find that our rooms were occupied and would not be available until later that morning. It was barely dawn and about thirty holidaymakers, of all ages, had to wait uncomfortably in the hotel foyer for several hours without refreshment until breakfast became available at 9.00 a.m. We were finally allocated rooms but my friend and I were put into a small window-less room on the roof of the hotel with only a skylight to view the Italian sunshine. We were extremely disappointed and complained to our courier – who spoke only limited English – but to no avail as there were no free rooms. We persisted however, and after five days we were moved to a room with a view of a field and more hotels! (Janice Honman, born in 1949)

SKYTRAIN

In 1977 Freddie Laker's "Skytrain" started its service of low-fare flights from Gatwick to New York. The Government and British Airways opposed Laker's right to offer this service, but the Civil Aviation Authority and the High Court upheld the original decision to award a licence to Laker Airways. The success of "Skytrain" started a price war among other airlines.

> I flew from London to New York with Laker Airways in the summer of 1979. I couldn't choose my day of departure: tickets were available only for the next flight which wasn't fully booked, in my case two days later. The ticket price was just £70 one way, easily the cheapest available at the time. Laker

Following the energy crisis, the incease in the cost of fuel made package holidays more expensive. After 1973 many people decided to stay at home and domestic tourism grew at the expense of foreign holidays. Some tour operators collapsed, leaving their customers without holidays and out of pocket or stranded abroad unable to obtain flights home.

Ask friends or relatives to describe any experience of package holidays in the 1970s. Did they think that they were good value for money at the time? Find out about surcharges and how they affected the price of many holidays during the energy crisis.

A passenger ticket for Freddie Laker's Skytrain. What is the current fare for a flight from London to New York?

kept the cost low partly by cutting out all the extras – even my meal cost me an extra £1.75, and some passengers took sandwiches – and partly by ensuring that each flight was fully booked. (Frank Harper, born in 1951)

Find out what happened to Laker Airways.

SAFARI PARKS

In 1970 three large safari parks at Windsor, Woburn and Blair Drummond were opened to accompany the two already in existence at Longleat and Stapleford. The animals, particularly the lions, roaming in these parks, became instant attractions for thousands of tourists.

Some 150 lions now roam freely in British parkland . . . . The vast number of visitors to the parks – up to 6000 cars a day at peak periods at the larger safari parks – raises considerable problems, particularly the "bunching" together of the cars and the consequent

NEW PUBLIC HOLIDAYS

Two new days were declared additional public holidays:

The provision of Jan. 1 1974, as a bank holiday was made by means of a Royal Proclamation . . . .(*Keesing's Contemporary Archives*, January 1974)

Mr Michael Foot, then Secretary of State for Employment, announced that as from 1978 May Day would be a bank holiday, and that consultations would begin shortly with the Trades Union Congress, the Confederation of British Industry and the banks as to whether the May Day holiday should be fixed on May 1 or the first Monday in May . . . . (*Keesing's Contemporary Archives*, March 1978)

Why was it necessary for the Government to consult with the above named parties?

discomfort of the passengers, who feel the need to open windows, which is strictly against regulations. (*The Year Book, 1971*, Book Club Associates)

Which other "theme" parks opened in the 1970s?

39

The Consumer Society

Unprecedented spending power in the early 1970s meant that customers were able to take full advantage of the large range of goods on offer. The economic recession, following a sharp rise in oil prices in 1973, brought an end to this. With the advent of shopping centres and hypermarkets, many customers were persuaded to change their shopping habits.

SHOPPING CENTRES

The following extract describes a proposed new development in Peterborough:

> **The project, known as the Queen Street Centre, will be built on a 15-acre site within the shadow of the cathedral and at present estimates will cost more than £15m [million]. The complex will be covered and air-conditioned. It will contain a department store, three variety stores, a fashion store, two supermarkets and about 80 shops. It will also incorporate pubs, cafés and restaurants, and possibly a club and discotheque with offices above the shops.** (*The Times*, 20 November 1975)

Shopping centres were and still are popular because they provide convenient parking and a variety of amenities in a covered traffic-free area. Some towns have closed central streets to traffic so that pedestrians can shop in safety. Small local tradesmen often suffered, however, as a result of these new developments.

Has your town a shopping centre or pedestrian precinct? Find out when it was built and if there was any local opposition to the development.

Many hypermarkets or superstores were built on the outskirts of towns in the 1970s. These enormous single-storey buildings provide many departments under one roof. They are usually surrounded by large car parks which allow trolleys to be unloaded directly into customers' cars.

The Office of Fair Trading was established in November 1973 to protect the consumer and the honest trader against unfair trading practices. The National Consumer Council, set up in February 1975, was mainly intended to put forward the customer's viewpoint where representation was necessary, especially to local authorities and the Government.

CONSUMER ADVICE

The 1970s saw more public awareness of consumer rights. As part of their response to this, many local authorities set up departments to advise consumers or deal with complaints. Christine Edmunds was appointed a Consumer Advisory Officer for Avon in 1976. Here she describes some aspects of her work:

> **To begin with the department was run on a shoe-string budget with only two officers working at a time. It was never**

necessary to advertise the service as we dealt with literally hundreds of complaints and on some days the phone would never stop ringing. We were not legally obliged to deal with all customer complaints, only those that involved criminal offences. Investigating complaints about new gadgets such as videos and digital watches took up a lot of our time. Some traders tended to become very suspicious of us and on one occasion when I was investigating a complaint a shopkeeper told me that I was worse than a traffic warden!
(Christine Edmunds, born in 1952)

Enquire at your local library or Town Hall about the consumer services that were available in your area in the 1970s.

CONSUMER COMPLAINTS

Many T.V. and radio programmes had a regular consumer feature dealing with complaints. In May 1974 the London magazine *Time Out* listed the following programmes as part of a feature advising the customer how to complain:

BBC Radio London, David Simmons, every other Thursday.
BBC Radio 4, Checkpoint.
BBC Radio 4, You and Yours, Wednesday.
BBC Radio 2, The Jimmy Young Show, daily.
BBC TV That's Life, Saturday.
BBC TV Nationwide, weekly.
Thames TV Good Afternoon, every other Friday. (*Time Out*, May 1974)

Do you recognize some of these programmes? Which other names could you add to the list today?

This special offer of "double stamps" was used to promote International Stores. Towards the end of the decade, the use of trading stamps had declined, as retailers concentrated on price competition instead. Which would you prefer – trading stamps or a price reduction?.

TRADING STAMPS

Some supermarkets and petrol stations gave trading stamps to their customers as an incentive for them to buy their goods. Once a shopper had filled a special book with these stamps he could either cash it in or exchange it for a gift.

Supermarket chains are bracing themselves today for an unparalleled price war. The High Street battle begins tomorrow when Tesco shops unveil their promised bargains in the wake of the group's decision to drop Green Shield Stamps . . . . Meanwhile, Tesco's rivals are planning counter-attacks. International Stores have taken up 100 of the Green Shield franchises left vacant when Tesco pulled out a month ago. They announced that they would be giving double stamps on every item. (*Daily Mail*, 8 June 1977)

What effect might this price war have had on small shops?

Concern for the Environment

The 1970s saw a growing concern for the environment. Many pressure groups were formed, and some became powerful social forces, successfully persuading both the public and government to be more aware of conservation. Scientists predicted that conventional energy sources would be exhausted before the next century. Alternative sources such as wind, wave and solar energy were developed. Some people worried about the use of nuclear power. They were concerned about the disposal of radioactive waste and the long-term health of those working and living near nuclear power stations.

SEVEN SISTERS COUNTRY PARK

Many national areas were conserved, not only to protect the landscape and wildlife but also to provide leisure amenities for the general public. One example of this is the Seven Sisters Country Park, which was acquired by East Sussex County Council in 1971. A leaflet issued by the council states its objectives:

> ... to conserve the scenic beauty, relative remoteness and wildlife; ... to provide opportunities for people to enjoy and appreciate its qualities .... Policies for the management follow from these objectives, such as banning motor vehicles from other than the car parks, and zoning the Park on an environmental basis to prevent damage by over-use to the more sensitive areas.

Greenpeace is an international organization which aims to halt what it calls "environmental abuse". This promotional material is from some of the group's many campaigns of the 1970s.

THE ECOLOGY PARTY

The Ecology Party is a political party that was created in the 1970s. It took a long while to grow but by 1979 *The Spectator* was able to describe it in the following terms:

> ... from being just another fringe movement they have suddenly taken up position as the fourth party in English politics. Their success in putting up over 50 candidates in the general election almost out of the blue and in obtaining a considerably higher vote, on average, than the 303 National Front candidates has already led to a nearly tripled membership [this was 3000]. (*The Spectator*, 2 June 1979)

What is the Ecology Party known as today? Your library will help you. Look in old copies of local newspapers to see if any Ecology candidates stood for election in your area during the 1970s. How many votes did they receive?

This photograph of the steel works in Corby, Northamptonshire, taken in 1978, shows the kind of environment that many people were concerned about in the 1970s. What appear to be the factors that caused their concern?

POLLUTION

The Royal Commission on Environmental Pollution issued a report in September 1972, dealing with pollution in some British estuaries and coastal waters. They found that:

> **a great and increasing volume of pollutants, some toxic, are reaching estuaries not only from rivers, but also by direct discharge .... There was too little protection from Parliament against industrial waste being put into the sea .... There should be a national policy for waste disposal, whereby waste products were not so much put where there was least control, but rather where they did least harm.**
> (*Whitaker's Almanack*, 1973)

The Commission recommended that there should be new legislation to control these discharges and therefore avoid more pollution.

If you live near the coast you could find out if water pollution was a problem in your area in the 1970s. There might be reports in local newspapers or in the minutes of council meetings. What opinions about the pollution might be held by the following people: naturalists, fishermen, those working in the tourist industry and those responsible for the discharge of the industrial waste?

RECYCLING

Friends of the Earth, a leading environmental pressure organization, was established in Britain in 1971. The following extract, taken from one of their information leaflets, describes how they drew public attention to the idea of recycling:

> **Friends of the Earth first hit the headlines in 1971 by dumping 1500 throwaway bottles on the doorstep of Schweppes, the soft drinks people. With no money or public support, Friends of the Earth had hit on one of the best ways of reaching a wide audience .... A new word – "recycling" – became part of our language ...**

What products are recycled today apart from glass? What are the environmental issues of today? Have they changed since the 1970s?

Difficult Words

age of majority	age of 18 at which most basic rights are granted to young people.
automation	the manufacture of a product by a machine.
bill	the draft of a proposed Act of Parliament.
comprehensive school	a local secondary school which provides education for all pupils of all abilities.
consumer	the buyer and user of an article or a service.
courier	employee of travel firm making arrangements at holiday destination.
devolution	the giving of work or power to another.
discrimination	unfair legal, social or economic treatment of a particular group.
franchise	privilege or right granted to a person or company.
high-rise tower	a building consisting of many storeys.
hypermarket	a very large single-storey building containing departments selling a variety of items.
immigrant	a person who has entered and settled in another country from their native land.
inflation	a situation in which prices rise and money loses its value.
legislation	the enacting of laws.
martial arts	Oriental unarmed combat.
meditation	an exercise in mental contemplation.
micro-chip	a tiny piece of silicon on which electronic circuits are printed.
mugging	the robbery and/or the physical attack of an individual in a public place.
nostalgia	sentimental yearning for the past.
organic farming	the farming of crops without the use of chemical pesticides, fertilizers, weed-killers, etc.
pressure group	an organization that hopes by its actions to influence the policies of other groups.
recession	a slow-down in trade and in the production of goods.
recycling	using valuable raw materials for a second time.
redeployment	moving an employee from one position to another within the same organization.
referendum	the act of letting the electorate decide a single political question by a general vote.
refugee	a person who is forced to leave their country and seek refuge in another.
state of emergency	a government declaration of a state of crisis in which special measures are needed.
terrorist	someone who uses violent methods to coerce a government or community.

CONVERSION TABLE

NEW MONEY		OLD MONEY
1p	=	2.4d. (2.4 old pence)
5p	=	1s. (1 shilling)
50p	=	10s. (10 shillings)
£1	=	£1
		12d=1 shilling
		20 shillings=£1
£1.05	=	21 shillings (a guinea)

1970 First major oilfield (the "Forties") discovered in the North Sea.
Labour Party loses General Election. Conservative Edward Heath becomes Prime Minister.
Eighteen-year-olds able to vote for the first time.
Brazil wins World Cup.

1971 Sixty-six spectators crushed to death in football disaster at Ibrox Park, Glasgow.
Idi Amin takes control of Uganda by military coup.
British postal workers on official strike for seven weeks.
Decimalization is introduced in Britain.
Population of Britain recorded as 55,364,551 on Census Day.
Heaviest rioting for 50 years in Northern Ireland as British government announces internment without trial for suspected terrorists.
House of Commons votes in favour of joining Common Market.
Publication of Local Government Bill reorganizing the counties of Britain.
War between India and Pakistan.

1972 Strategic Arms Limitation Treaty (S.A.L.T. 1) is signed by United States and Russia.
Unemployment in Britain reaches one million.
State of Emergency declared because of power crisis.
Britain imposes direct rule from Westminster on Northern Ireland.
Burglars caught in Watergate building, U.S. Democrat Party campaign headquarters.
Idi Amin expels 40,000 British Asians from Uganda. They flee to Britain.
Seventeen people die in Palestinian terrorist attack at Munich Olympics.
Sir John Betjeman succeeds Cecil Day Lewis as Poet Laureate.
Richard Nixon elected for further term as U.S. President.
1.6 million people visit Tutankhamun Exhibition at British Museum.

1973 Britain, Denmark and Ireland join Common Market.
Last U.S. troops leave Vietnam.
Value Added Tax (V.A.T.) is introduced.
Watergate cover-up in U.S. begins to be exposed.
Middle East War breaks out. Oil prices rise rapidly in a few weeks.
Princess Anne marries Captain Mark Phillips.
I.R.A. bomb attacks on British cities.
Britain is reduced to a three-day working week because of the energy crisis and miners' strike.

1974 Conservatives lose General Election in February. Harold Wilson becomes Prime Minister for the third time but without an overall majority. Labour wins second General Election in October.
Nurses begin a series of strikes for more pay.
West Germany wins World Cup.
Nixon resigns as U.S. President. Gerald Ford replaces him.
Twenty-one killed, 120 hurt in Birmingham pub bombings.

1975 Edward Heath beaten by Margaret Thatcher for leadership of Conservative Party.
End of Vietnam War.
Britain votes in referendum to stay in Common Market.
Department of Energy launches its "SAVE-IT" campaign.
"Spaghetti House" siege in London ends with release of unharmed hostages.

1976 Concorde flights begin.
James Callaghan succeeds Harold Wilson as Prime Minister.
Britain starts exporting North Sea oil.
Jeremy Thorpe resigns as Liberal leader; David Steel succeeds him.
Emergency powers to control water shortage, caused by worst British drought for centuries.
Unemployment tops one and a half million.
Chairman Mao dies in China.
British Rail introduces High Speed Trains.
Jimmy Carter elected as U.S. President.

1977 Britain celebrates Silver Jubilee.
Labour pact with Liberals enables Government to win 'no confidence' vote in House of Commons.
Grunwick industrial dispute.
Kerry Packer forms his alternative series of cricket matches.
Virginia Wade wins Ladies' Singles Championship at Wimbledon.
First cheap Skytrain flights take place.
Firemen strike; members of the Armed Forces deal with fires.

1978 Amoco Cadiz oil tanker disaster occurs.
Radio broadcasting of Parliament starts.
Argentina wins World Cup.

First test-tube baby is born in Britain.
Ford strike on pay dispute.
Unrest grows in Iran.

1979 Many strikes cause "winter of discontent".
Shah flees Iran. Ayatollah Khomeini returns from exile to form republic.
Referendums on Welsh and Scottish devolution.
Airey Neave, Conservative spokesman on N. Ireland, assassinated by I.N.L.A.
Lord Mountbatten assassinated by I.R.A.

S.A.L.T. 2 agreement signed by U.S. and Russia.
First direct elections to European Parliament.
Idi Amin flees Uganda.
Iranian students hold U.S. Embassy officials hostage.
Sir Anthony Blunt named as a former spy.
Russian troops occupy Afghanistan.
Final agreement on future of Rhodesia signed.
Vietnamese government expels ethnic Chinese people from Vietnam.

Biographical Notes

ASHLEY, Laura (1925-85). Born in Glamorgan. Began by designing fabrics, then opened first shop in Kensington, London, in 1967. Designed and sold Victorian-style print dresses made of natural fabrics. Many of her designs were inspired by visits to European museums. With her husband Bernard as business partner she expanded her merchandise from clothes and fabrics into wallpaper and soft furnishings. Died in 1985 as a result of injuries sustained in a fall. There were 180 Laura Ashley shops worldwide at the time of her death.

CALLAGHAN, Sir James (born 1912). Worked for the Inland Revenue when he left school. Became Labour M.P. for Cardiff South in 1945. Worked at the Ministry of Transport, where he was responsible for safety measures such as cats' eyes and zebra crossings. Held offices of Chancellor of the Exchequer, Home Secretary and Foreign Secretary before succeeding Harold Wilson as Leader of the Labour Party and Prime Minister in 1976. Made a member of the Order of the Garter in 1987.

CONRAN, Sir Terence (born 1931). Opened the first Habitat shop in 1964 to sell the best modern designs in Europe. Gradually expanded the business until it grew into a very successful international chain of shops. Conran is now chairman of the Habitat Mothercare Public Company which is one of the largest retail organizations in the world. He has won several prestigious design awards. Publications include *The House Book* (1974), *The Kitchen Book* (1977) and *The Bedroom and Bathroom Book* (1978). Knighted in 1983.

HEATH, Edward (born 1916). Educated at Oxford. Became Conservative M.P. for Bexley, Kent in 1950. Prime Minister 1970-4. Took Britain into the E.E.C. in January 1973. Led Opposition until 1975 when he was succeeded by Margaret Thatcher. Refused to serve in her Shadow Cabinet and retired to the back benches.

LAKER, Sir Freddie (born 1922). Began his career as an entrepreneur after the Second World War, when he bought and sold converted bombers. Also sold aircraft scrap and launched the first cross-Channel air ferry. Set up his own airline in 1966. This expanded through deals with tour operators. Took six years from 1971 to 1977 for him to win a license allowing him to operate his cut-rate walk-on Skytrain flights across the Atlantic. Knighted in 1978. Following Laker's success, larger airlines began introducing economy flights. This eventually put Skytrain out of business.

MARK, Sir Robert (born 1917). A distinguished career in the police force led to his appointment as Commissioner of the Metropolitan Police from 1972 to 1977. Had the difficult task of combatting the wave of bombings, shootings and violent crimes in London at that time and of ridding the force of corruption. Two notable successes were the capture without loss of life of the three gunmen involved in the "Spaghetti House Siege" and the four I.R.A. terrorists in the "Balcombe Street Siege". He has written two books, *Policing a Perplexed Society* (1977) and *In the Office of Constable* (1978).

MONTY PYTHON TEAM. Five Oxford and Cambridge graduates – Graham Chapman, John Cleese, Michael Palin, Terry Jones and Eric Idle – and one American, Terry Gilliam, responsible for *Monty Python's Flying Circus* T.V. comedy series shown by the B.B.C. in the early 1970s. Films made by the team include *Monty Python and the Holy Grail* and *Monty Python's Life of Brian.* The team no longer work together, but during the late 1970s individual members were responsible for *Fawlty Towers* (John Cleese), *Ripping Yarns* (Michael Palin and Terry Jones), *Rutland Weekend Television* (Eric Idle), all for the B.B.C., and the film *Jabberwocky* (Terry Gilliam). Other members of the team continue to write, perform and direct.

MOUNTBATTEN, Lord Louis (1900-79) Great-grandson of Queen Victoria and uncle to Prince Philip. A professional sailor who served during the First and Second World Wars. Appointed Supreme Allied Commander, South-East Asia in 1943 and last Viceroy of India in 1947 with the task of overseeing the transition to independence. Assassinated along with other members of his family by the I.R.A. in 1979.

SINCLAIR, Sir Clive (born 1940). Worked as a technical journalist before founding his own firm in 1962 selling radio and amplifier kits. Rapid expansion took him to Cambridge and earned him a reputation as an electronics pioneer. His innovations in the 1970s included the digital watch and the pocket calculator. In 1980 his company Sinclair Research launched its first personal computer – Sinclair ZX80 – the first in the world to retail for under £100. Knighted in 1983. His more recent invention, the C5 electric vehicle, was not a success.

STEEL, David (born 1938). Born in Scotland and educated in Nairobi, Kenya and at Edinburgh University. He has been a journalist and a broadcaster as well as a

46

politician. Entered Parliament in 1965 as Liberal M.P. for Roxburgh, Selkirk and Peebles. Liberal Chief Whip 1970-5. Succeeded Jeremy Thorpe as Leader of the Liberal Party in 1976 and helped to unite the Liberal Party after months of bitter internal disputes. Along with Dr David Owen he was joint leader of the S.D.P.-Liberal Aliance.

THATCHER, Margaret (born 1925). Born in Grantham, Lincolnshire, where her family owned a grocer's shop. Studied chemistry at Oxford and later became a barrister. Conservative M.P. for Finchley, North London from 1959. As Secretary of State for Education and Science when the Conservatives were in power 1970-4 she was responsible for stopping free milk for 8-11 year olds. This controversial piece of legislation earned her the nickname "Margaret Thatcher, milk snatcher". Succeeded Edward Heath as Leader of the Conservative Party in 1975 and in 1979 became Britain's first woman Prime Minister. Re-elected to second term of office in 1983, and third term in 1987.

WILSON, Sir Harold (born 1916). Educated at Oxford where he won first class honours in Philosophy, Politics and Economics. Became Labour M.P. for Ormskirk, Lancashire 1945-50 and Huyton 1950-83. Elected Leader of the Labour Party in 1963 and was Prime Minister 1964-70 and 1974-6. He resigned in 1976 and was created a Baron in 1983.

Book List

Books for Younger Readers

Edwards, John, *The Seventies*, Macdonald Educational, 1980

Fyson, Nance Lui, *Growing Up in the 1970s*, Batsford, 1980

Books for Older Readers

Allison, Ronald, *Britain in the Seventies*, Country Life Books, 1980

Bartlett, C.J., *A History of Post-War Britain 1945-1974*, Longman, 1977

Booker, Christopher, *The Seventies, Portrait of a Decade*, Allen Lane, 1980

Madgwick, P.J., Steeds, D. and Williams, L.J., *Britain Since 1945*, Hutchinson, 1982

Shrapnel, Norman, *The Seventies, Britain's Inward March*, Constable and Company Ltd, 1980

Wilmot, Roger, *From Fringe to Flying Circus*, Eyre Methuen, 1980

Acknowledgments

The Author and Publishers would like to thank the following for their kind permission to reproduce illustrations: BBC Hulton Picture Library, pages 10, 14, 18, 21, 30, 43 and cover (top); Consumers' Association, publishers of *Which?*, page 25; *The Guardian*, page 7; Greenpeace, page 42; London Borough of Bromley, cover (bottom left); London Borough of Camden, page 19; London Express News and Features Services, pages 12 and 32; Habitat, page 35; Inca, page 34; Kentish Times Newspapers, page 8 and frontispiece; *Private Eye*, page 24; *Punch*, page 29; Simplicity Patterns Ltd, page 5 and cover (bottom right).

The Author and Publishers would also like to thank all those authors, journals and publishers who gave permission to reproduce written sources. In addition they would like to thank: Chappell Music, for "Imagine" by John Lennon © 1971 Lenono Music, page 37; The Controller of Her Majesty's Stationery Office, pages 13, 18 and 29; Curtis Brown Ltd, for kind permission to reprint material © Christopher Booker 1980, pages 21 and 22; *Daily Mirror*, page 41; Friends of the Earth, pages 25 and 43; Kentish Times Newspapers for material from the *Bromley Times* and *Chislehurst Times*, pages 6, 9, 10, 12, 29 and 32; Mail Newspapers plc, page 41.

Additional photographs were taken by Frank Harper. The map on page 44 was drawn by R.F. Brien.

Index